SCR

The
Lord
Is My
Shepherd

❧ *Psalm 23* ❧

MELANNIE SVOBODA, SND

Living with Christ Books

To Lou Alexander,
my dear friend, who loved
and followed the Good Shepherd
all the days of her life.

TWENTY-THIRD PUBLICATIONS
A Division of Bayard
One Montauk Avenue, Suite 200 » New London, CT 06320
(860) 437-3012 or (800) 321-0411
www.23rdpublications.com

ISBN: 978-1-62785-112-1
Library of Congress Control Number: 2015947542
Printed in the U.S.A.

❧ CONTENTS ❧

It's short.

It uses simple words.

It offers striking imagery.

It exudes profound trust in God.

Little wonder that Psalm 23 is one of the most cherished and frequently recited prayers of all times. It is chosen by couples for their weddings. It is sung by mourners at the funerals of their loved ones. And it is one of the first prayers we teach our children.

Despite its traditional popularity, Psalm 23 does not appeal to everyone today. Some people have a hard time being compared to sheep, those smelly and simpleminded animals. Others say the world we live in today is too far removed from the shepherd's world to make this psalm relevant. After all, what do we know about raising sheep or working in pastures? We are more apt to be raising children and working long hours in offices, factories, stores, or homes. Chances are we are not worrying about predators as much as we are worrying about the future for our families, our country, our church, and our world. And seldom do we have the luxury anymore of strolling through green pastures. More often than not we're speeding along on expressways or standing in long checkout lines. And we don't drink our water from running streams or still waters anymore, but from kitchen spigots or plastic bottles. Given our current circumstances, can this prayer still speak to us today?

Yes it can. Definitely! And this small book attempts to show how Psalm 23 is as relevant today as it was when it was first uttered many centuries ago. We will begin with a few words on the origin of the psalm. Then we will take the psalm line by line, offering some thoughts on the meaning and significance of that line for us today. At the end of each chapter are some questions for personal reflection, journaling, or group sharing. Each chapter concludes with a short prayer that grows out of the reflection. It is my hope that these simple reflections on Psalm 23 may touch your mind and your heart, leading you ever closer to the Shepherd who loves you more than you can imagine.

BACKGROUND

Where did this psalm come from? Who wrote it? And when? We don't know. At least not for sure. But for centuries Psalm 23 has been attributed to David, the great king of Israel who lived from 1040 to 970 BC. It's easy to see why he is linked to this psalm. David was known as Israel's "Shepherd King"; and before becoming king, David was indeed a shepherd boy. Furthermore, as he watched over his sheep, David often strummed his lyre (a forerunner of the guitar) to pass the time away. Over time he gained a reputation for composing beautiful songs, most of them religious in nature. David's songs were so powerful and faith-filled that they helped to dispel the "dark moods" that plagued Saul, the first king of Israel.

Though we may not be able to name with absolute certainty *who* composed Psalm 23, we do know *what kind of a person* the author was. The author was someone well acquainted with life's sorrows and joys—with life's dark valleys and green pastures. The author had experienced life's pains and pleasures, the thickets that ensnare and cut as well as the lush green grass that offers rest and repose. The author knew evil and goodness. He had enemies eyeing him with suspicion and even hatred; but he also had the "Shepherd" gazing upon him with love and tenderness. As we shall see, the author of Psalm 23 was sensitive, humble, grateful, and joyful. But most of all, the author was someone trying to walk with God each day, trying to follow God's promptings, and trying to trust in God no matter what.

I think it's fairly safe to say that the author of Psalm 23 was a lot like us.

PSALM 23

The Lord is my shepherd;
*   there is nothing I lack.*
In green pastures you let me graze;
*   to safe waters you lead me;*
*   you restore my strength.*
You guide me along the right path
*   for the sake of your name.*
Even when I walk through a dark valley,
*   I fear no harm for you are at my side;*
*   your rod and staff give me courage.*

You set a table before me
*   as my enemies watch;*
You anoint my head with oil;
*   my cup overflows.*
Only goodness and love will pursue me
*   all the days of my life;*
I will dwell in the house of the Lord
*   for years to come.*

(NEW AMERICAN BIBLE, 1970 EDITION)

ONE

The Lord is my shepherd

INTIMACY WITH GOD

To appreciate Psalm 23, we must first know something about sheep and shepherds. Let's begin with the sheep. One outstanding characteristic of sheep is this: they are extremely vulnerable. That's because sheep have few natural defenses. They have no sharp teeth, no claws, and no speed or agility. They are not particularly intelligent either. Because of their vulnerability, they tend to flock together for security. But if they sense danger, they often panic and scatter in all directions. This scattering makes them easy prey for predators. As someone has said, "A lone sheep is a sitting duck."

Sheep need someone to watch over them just to survive. They need a shepherd. A *good* shepherd. What are some of the qualities of a good shepherd? First of all, a good shepherd knows his sheep—as a flock and as individuals. He knows their strengths and their weaknesses. He knows their needs, preferences, and fears. Conversely, the sheep know their shepherd. They know his voice, his touch, and even his scent.

How are the images of sheep and shepherd relevant for us living in the twenty-first century? We are like sheep in our vulnerability. In recent years our vulnerability has been underscored in countless ways. Every day we are bombarded with stories of violence, war, terrorism, global warming, viral epidemics, and natural disasters of all kinds. We experience our economic vulnerability too. A military coup anywhere in the world can cause global stock markets to plummet or gas prices to skyrocket. As individuals, we experience our vulnerability whenever we are touched by illness—either our own or that of a loved one. In addition, we experience the vulnerability that often accompanies the natural aging process, including stiff joints, reduced energy levels, diminishment of sight or hearing, and memory lapses. And finally, we feel our vulnerability every time we fail in our continuous efforts to do the right thing. Yes, the vulnerable sheep in Psalm 23 is an apt image for vulnerable us. We need someone to protect and care for us. We need a shepherd. We need God.

That's what Psalm 23 proclaims: our need for God. But the psalm does more than remind us of this need. It tells us what our relationship with God truly is. Notice that the psalmist says, "The Lord is *my* shepherd." He does not say, "The Lord is *our* shepherd." The word *my* implies a personal relationship. A *mutual* personal relationship. I belong to the shepherd, but the shepherd belongs to me too. The Quaker teacher Douglas Steere said that the ancient question, "Who am I?" leads inevitably to the equally important question, "*Whose* am I?" This psalm answers that question: "I am God's."

Faith, then, is not primarily an intellectual assent to certain dogmas. Nor is it mere obedience to particular rules. Faith is first and foremost a personal relationship with God, with Jesus, and with the Spirit. Faith is intimacy with the Divine. Psalm 23 celebrates this faith, this intimacy. It is a prayer of assurance: God watches over us as a shepherd watches over his sheep—tenderly, carefully, constantly. But Psalm 23 is not a prayer of cheap assurance. It offers no rose-colored glasses.

It does not say: If we have faith, we will be invulnerable.

It does not say: If we have faith, our life with be problem free.

It does not say: If we have faith, everything in our life will make sense.

No, Psalm 23 says: Even when we experience our vulnerability in frightening ways, even when we encounter adversities on all sides, and even when our life makes absolutely no sense, *God is with us.*

And (as we will see) God is with us not as an outside observer but as our intimate partner. God is with us not as harsh critic but as gentle guide. God is with us not as the fixer of our daily problems but as the provider of our deepest needs.

Psalm 23 is a prayer for vulnerable people. That's all of us. It is a prayer for people striving to know the shepherd more and more each day. And how do we do that? The same way we come to know any person: by spending time with them. This means setting time aside to be with God in prayer. Bishop Robert Morneau reminds us that there are 144 10-minute segments in every day. Are we willing to give God one or two of them?

And when we pray, what do we talk to God about? Everything! Nothing is too big or too small. Nothing is off limits. We don't have to worry about using the right words either. In this regard, we can learn a lot about prayer from children. A four-year-old boy prayed: "Dear God, I love you with all my heart and guts." Now that's a great prayer! An eight-year-old girl prayed: "I think about you sometimes, God, even when I'm not praying." That's solid spirituality!

Intimacy with God can include pondering God's word—as you are doing right now. It can also entail sharing our thoughts and experiences with other "sheep," that is, with other believers. Primarily, though, intimacy with God means keeping the shepherd within our sight, listening for the shepherd's voice, and following the shepherd's scent as we walk the green pastures and dark valleys of our life.

Someone has said the most important word in Psalm 23 is the fourth word: *my*. Reciting this prayer regularly will help us to say with ever growing conviction: "Yes, the Lord really is *my* shepherd."

QUESTIONS

1. Recall a time when you felt particularly weak or vulnerable. How did you feel? Did you turn to someone for help? Did you turn to God?

2. What kind of things do you talk to God about in prayer? Why? Are there some things you never talk to God about? Why not?

PRAYER

Divine Shepherd,
you are *my* shepherd.
I belong to you and you belong to me.
I need you. Desperately.
In so many ways I am weak and vulnerable.
But the good news is this: I have you.

And you know me.
You are familiar with all my ways.
You know my weaknesses, my strengths,
	my preferences, my fears.
Help me to become more familiar
	with *your* ways,
through my daily conversations with you,
my pondering of your holy word,
and my reflecting on the people
	and events of my daily life.
Draw me to ever greater intimacy with you,
my Shepherd, *my* Beloved One.
Amen.

There is nothing I lack

BALANCING CONTENTMENT
AND RESTLESSNESS

This line from Psalm 23 has been translated in many different ways:

"There is nothing I lack."

"I shall not want."

"I have all that I need."

"I will not be without any good thing."

No matter how you translate the line, the words imply a deep contentment with life. This contentment is a direct outgrowth of the verse that precedes this one: *The Lord is my shepherd.* I am content in life because I have my shepherd.

And having God in my life far outweighs anything else I could want.

But holding up contentment as a goal in the spiritual life can be dangerous. Why? Because contentment, carried to extreme, can morph into undesirable qualities such as passivity, lethargy, and even apathy. So when we pray this line, we must simultaneously remind ourselves of these great truths:

Discontent at times can be a good thing.

Longing and desires can be holy.

Restlessness can be a great grace.

How can this be? Discontentment, longing, and restlessness are all blessings if they draw us or even drive us to God. For God alone can fulfill the deepest desires of our hearts. Isn't this what St. Augustine meant when he wrote, "Our hearts are restless, O Lord, until they rest in Thee"? I suspect this is also what St. Paul had in mind when he reminded the Philippians that they were "not citizens of earth." In other words, earth is not our final home; therefore, the deepest longings of our hearts cannot be satisfied here. Instead, we are innately restless.

Pope Francis spoke in positive terms about this restlessness. In a homily on the feast of St. Augustine, he said, "Do not get comfortable in the Christian life. Be restless...be restless in proclaiming the Lord with courage. Be restless in your love for every brother and sister."

The great challenge of the spiritual life, then, is this: How do we balance the contentment spoken of in Psalm 23 with the holy restlessness of which Augustine and others speak? We can get help to do this in several ways.

First, we can look to Jesus. Jesus encouraged the kind of contentment spoken about in Psalm 23. He said, "Fear not, little flock." Ultimately, we have nothing to be afraid of because we have Jesus our Shepherd. Jesus also directed our innate restlessness with words such as these: "Come to me...and I will give you rest." Jesus displayed his own contentment when he described his mission in life: "My food is to do the will of the one who sent me." And in the Garden of Gethsemane, when Judas and a large crowd arrived to arrest him, Jesus, with amazing calm and composure, said to his disciples: "The hour has come...Get up, let us go. See, my betrayer is at hand."

At the same time, Jesus warned against lethargy and apathy. He held up for emulation individuals who took action: the good Samaritan caring for the robbery victim on the side of the road, the Roman soldier interceding for his sick servant, the destitute widow tossing her two coins into the temple treasury, and the nameless woman anointing him with costly nard shortly before his death. Jesus described the final judgment in terms of doing good deeds: feeding the hungry, clothing the naked, giving drink to the thirsty, visiting the imprisoned. As the old maxim says, "Be not simply good; be good for something."

The example of the saints can also help us learn to balance contentment and restlessness. St. Francis of Assisi divested himself of material wealth and was content to live a life of poverty. But he didn't just sit around talking to the birds. He devoted his time and energies to "repairing the church" as God had directed him to do. St. Teresa of Avila encouraged contentment in her sisters. The bookmark in her prayer book said, "Let nothing disturb you...God alone suffices." At the same time, she was very disturbed by the laxity she saw in many of the convents and monasteries around her. As a result, she set out to reform the Carmelite order of her day. Closer to our own day, Blessed Katharine Drexel displayed her absolute trust in the Shepherd by divesting herself of her substantial family wealth. Simultaneously, she was discontented with the church's neglect of Native Americans and African Americans, so she founded a religious congregation devoted to serving them.

Many spiritual writers have written eloquently on the blessing inherent in our restlessness and discontent. The great theologian Karl Rahner, SJ, wrote of the "insufficiency of everything attainable." In this life, he said, "all symphonies remain unfinished." Even children can experience the insufficiency of everything attainable. I am reminded of a cartoon I saw a while back. It showed a little boy on Christmas morning right after he has torn open all his presents. As he sits in a sea of toys, boxes, ribbons, and wrapping paper, he says to his parents, "Is this all there is?" As adults, we too experience the ache for more; as believers, we know that this earthly life is *not* all there is!

There is nothing I lack. Yes, we can pray these words because we have our Shepherd. And in having our Shepherd, we have all we need. Yet we also know that the discontent, longings, and restlessness we feel at times will draw us ever closer to that Divine Shepherd and to one another—if we allow them to.

QUESTIONS

1. Name a time when you felt restless or discontented. What did you do with these feelings? Name a time when you experienced deep contentment. What factors contributed to this feeling?

---

2. Have any of your deepest longings ever been an impetus for prayer or for good works? If so, in what way?

PRAYER

Beloved Shepherd,
when I'm feeling lonely,
remind me: I have you.

When I'm feeling empty,
remind me: I have you.
When I'm feeling restless,
remind me: I have you.
When I'm feeling fearful,
remind me: I have you.
When I'm beset with problems,
remind me: I have you.
When I'm feeling sad,
remind me: I have you.
When I'm feeling discouraged,
remind me: I have you.
When I'm feeling jealous,
remind me: I have you.

Channel my discontent into doing
    good deeds for others.
Channel my longings into the desire
    to know you better.
Channel my restlessness into ever greater
    trust in you.
And finally, my beloved Shepherd,
keep reminding me: In having you,
I ultimately have all I need. Amen.

THREE

In green pastures you let me graze

CELEBRATING THE SABBATH

S omeone has said, "Green must be one of God's favorite colors—because there's so much of it in our world." Yes, green is certainly a pervasive color in nature. Trees, bushes, grass, certain precious gems, and even some frogs (like Kermit) are green. Green is also a popular color for interior decorating. We often paint the walls of our homes, schools, hospitals, hotels, and even prisons green. Why? Maybe it's because recent studies have shown that soft green colors promote calm and tranquility.

This verse from Psalm 23 speaks of green pastures. But a careful reading of the line shows that it is not about the shepherd providing *food* for the sheep. Rather, it is about the shepherd providing a safe place for the sheep to rest, a place of calm and tranquility. The King James translation expresses this concept more clearly: "He makes me to lie down in green pastures." The image is not of sheep eating; it is of sheep resting.

Sheep tend to be skittish, so it is not easy to get them to lie down and rest. Sometimes it is not easy to get humans to lie down and rest either. As we pray this verse from the psalm, we might want to ask ourselves: What aspects of my life cause me to be fretful or agitated? Perhaps we are working long hours just to make ends meet. Or maybe we are at odds with family members, coworkers, or neighbors. Or maybe we are bothered by bills to pay, car problems, the hectic pace of life, vexing circumstances, the vagaries of the weather, or the constant bombardment of bad news. Or perhaps our fretfulness is fueled by a wide range of unmet hungers—the hunger for greater financial security, deeper satisfaction in our work, or more appreciation from our family.

So what wisdom does this verse provide for us? For one thing, it reminds us that God wants us to rest. The words "He *makes me* to lie down..." suggest a gentle persuasion. This concept of regular rest was so important that it was enshrined in the Ten Commandments. The Third Commandment says, "Remember to keep holy the Sabbath." And precisely how were the Israelites instructed to keep the Sabbath holy? Primarily in two ways: by worshiping God and by refraining from work, that is, by resting and relaxing. Worshiping God seems an obvious way to make a day holy. But refraining from work? How does that consecrate the day? Simple. By letting go of their work on the Sabbath, the Israelites were demonstrating their trust in God, the author of all life and all labor. It was a concrete way for them to remember that even their work and the fruits of their work belonged to God.

The Sabbath restrictions on labor also provided time for the people to be with family and friends. This regular togetherness forged and strengthened familial and communal bonds. The spiritual writer Wilkie Au reminds us that leisure is a vital component of spirituality. He writes: "Any spirituality that leaves out leisure will lack depth and balance, because leisure lies at the heart of prayer, solitude, community, and friendship." Leisure, then, helps make the Sabbath holy.

One way to live this verse, then, is to reclaim this Sabbath tradition—that is, to let go of our work on a regular basis and give ourselves over to leisure activities that refresh us: going for a walk, enjoying a family meal, connecting with friends, playing with a child, reading a good book, visiting a park or zoo, engaging in a favorite sport, taking in a movie, play, or concert.

Another way to live this verse centers on that word *green:* We can celebrate the Sabbath by connecting with nature, making time to enjoy its rhythms, its beauty, and its mystery. Pope Francis, in his encyclical *Laudato Si,'* encourages us to do just that by reminding us that "soil, water, mountains: everything is...a caress from God." A while ago I came across a disturbing statistic: the average American spends ten minutes a day outside. Ten minutes! I fear we are becoming more and more an "indoor people." And if we are, then we risk becoming divorced from the natural world altogether. When this happens, we can begin to take that world for granted and fail to appreciate our interconnectedness with all that is. Such a lack of awareness can have dire consequences for the future of our planet. So one way to live this verse is to rest regularly in those "green pastures" of our beautiful world.

The example of Jesus can be our inspiration. Jesus worked very hard, but he also took time to rest. He cultivated friendship with his apostles and with Lazarus, Mary, Martha, Mary Magdalene, and Nicodemus, to name a few. He was profoundly connected with the natural world. The images he used in his teachings demonstrate his closeness with creation: water, grains of wheat, grape vines, mustard seeds, flowers, the birds of the air, fish, sheep, goats, camels, mother hens, and the list goes on. This is the Jesus who calls us regularly to "come aside and rest a while."

Some of us are lucky to have people in our life who encourage us to play. That reminds me of this classified ad from a small-town newspaper: "Retired school teacher, tired of reading, 'riting, and 'rithmetic. Is there a gentleman out there in his late sixties or older who can help me find my way to the playground before the bell rings?"

QUESTIONS

1. How do you try to "keep holy the Sabbath"?

2. Describe a time when you felt connected to the rhythm, beauty, or mystery of the natural world. What effect did this experience have on you?

PRAYER

Shepherd of the Sabbath,
when I am weary from my labors,
let me hear you say to me,
    "Come aside and rest a while."
When I am anxious and fearful
    about many things,
let me hear you say to me,
    "Come aside and rest a while."
When I am at odds with others or bothered
    by daily annoyances,

let me hear you say to me,
    "Come aside and rest a while."
When I am restless and hungry
    for things I cannot even name,
let me hear you say to me,
    "Come aside and rest a while."
Gently lead me to the green pastures
    you have provided for me.
Encourage me to rest and just be.
Impart to me a deep sense of your presence,
    your watchfulness, your care.
May my celebration of the Sabbath
give praise to your name.
May it help to forge the bonds
    of family and community.
And may my celebration of the Sabbath
reconnect me with the beautiful world
    you have fashioned for us.
I ask for these things through Jesus,
    who said to his disciples
on more than one occasion:
"Come aside and rest a while."
Amen.

FOUR

To safe waters you lead me

Drinking from Lifegiving Waters

To safe waters you lead me. One of the shepherd's main priorities is finding water for the sheep. The water must be *safe,* that is, not contaminated. As we pray Psalm 23, we might ask God for a renewed appreciation for water.

Even before we were born, we were dependent upon water. We lived and grew in water, the amniotic fluid of the womb. Rachel Carson, marine biologist and conservationist, described this reality beautifully in her book *The Sea Around*

Us. She said each of us began life "in a miniature ocean," our mother's womb. We went through the stages of embryonic development, repeating the steps by which the human race evolved: "from gill-breathing inhabitants of a water-world to creatures able to live on land."

After birth, our dependency on water continues. At birth a baby's body is composed of eighty percent water. As adults, it's seventy percent water. We can live without food for a month or so, but we can live without water for only about a week. Clean water is the basis for good health. Contaminated water, on the other hand, is the leading cause of illness and epidemics in parts of the world. Perhaps the anthropologist Loren Eiseley summarizes the importance of water best: "If there is magic on this planet, it is contained in water."

How can we renew our appreciation of water? We can begin by looking at some of the photographs of earth taken by the Apollo astronauts. Earth looks like a beautiful blue and white marble suspended against the blackness of space. We see that water covers most of the earth's surface (about seventy-one percent). And we know it is found in many forms: oceans, ice caps, clouds, rain, rivers, underground reservoirs (aquifers), lakes, ponds, wetlands, and dew.

We can also become more sensitive to the water we use every day. We can ask ourselves: Do we know and appreciate its source? Are we respectful of the water we use or do we take it for granted? Worse yet, do we waste this precious commodity? We can also affirm that water is a basic right for life, a right that is being threatened by several factors. First of all, its scarcity. Though water is plentiful on earth, less than three percent of it is freshwater and thus drinkable. And more than two-thirds of that three percent is frozen in glaciers and ice caps. That leaves less than one percent of all freshwater on earth to be used for human agriculture, industry, and communities.

This right to water is also being threatened by inequalities in its use. The average American, for example, uses one hundred and fifty-three gallons of water per day while the average Asian uses twenty-three gallons and the average African only twelve. In some parts of the world, hauling water consumes hours of valuable time each day.

The task of carrying water almost always falls to girls and women. Another factor that threatens peoples' basic right to water is increased privatization of water. In some places, private companies are claiming the rights to water sources for their manufacturing purposes, thus denying water to the surrounding community.

The issues of scarcity of water, inequalities in its use, and privatization may seem far removed from Psalm 23, but they aren't. In fact, this verse may be urging us to take a fresh look at this valuable resource and the particular challenges we face today.

What was Jesus' attitude toward water? Growing up in a land where water was often scarce, Jesus probably developed a high regard for water. As a child he may have gone to the well every morning with his mother to draw water for their day's use. Before beginning his public ministry, he stepped down into the waters of the Jordan River and was baptized by John the Baptist. Throughout his ministry, Jesus seemed drawn to the Sea of Galilee. In fact, it was on its shores that he called his first disciples and taught the multitudes. On several occasions, Jesus also showed he could control water. He changed water into wine, he calmed the chaotic storm at sea, and he actually walked on water.

But Jesus did more than appreciate and control water. He identified his teachings and even his very self with water. To the Samaritan woman at the well, he said, "Everyone who drinks from this water will be thirsty again; but whoever drinks the water I shall give will never thirst again." And shortly before he was arrested he told the crowds, "Let anyone who thirsts come to me and drink."

We need life-giving waters for our spiritual life too. One source of this water is God's word. Countless Christians rise early every morning to nourish themselves with this water, this "heavenly dew." Others pause some time during the day to drink from this source. Our Shepherd provides other sources of spiritual water for us: insights gleaned in our personal prayer, the Eucharist and other sacraments, family, friendship, the kindness of strangers, the service we give to one another, and the beauty and wonders of creation. Do I regularly take advantage of these spiritual waters?

The writer Brian Doyle describes water as "a graceful creature...sinuous and ungraspable, the first ingredient of life, the substance that composes, cleanses, rejuvenates us." He concludes: "Water is an apt metaphor for grace." We could also say water is an apt metaphor for God.

QUESTIONS

1. In what ways are you aware of the water you use on a given day: the water you drink, bathe or shower in, cook with, swim in, etc.? Do you ever waste this precious commodity? Take time to thank God for the gift of water.

2. What are your sources for water for your spiritual life? How do you drink from these sources?

PRAYER

Water...where all life first began.
Water...where I first began
in the miniature ocean of my mother's womb.
Water...70% of who I am.

Water...life giving...life forming...life sustaining.
Water...cleansing...healing...rejuvenating.
I thank you, Good Shepherd,
     for the gift of water:
for oceans, ice caps, clouds, rain, rivers,
     aquifers,
lakes, ponds, wetlands, and dew.
Let me never forget:
Clean water is the world's first medicine.
Clean water is the basic right of all people.
Clean water must never be taken for granted.
Help me to appreciate the spiritual waters
that refresh my soul:
Scripture, prayer, the sacraments,
family, friends, kindness, service,
     and the whole of creation.
Continue to lead me to safe waters,
     to still waters.
And may I, by the way I follow you,
lead others to these life-giving waters too.
I ask for these things through Jesus
and the power of his rejuvenating Spirit. Amen.

FIVE

You restore my strength

FORGIVENESS: CALLING FORTH INTO THE LIGHT

Steven, a kindergartner, slowly crawled into the car one afternoon appearing very sad. Since he usually jumps into his booster seat smiling and talking, his mother asked, "Is something wrong?" Then Steven told her what had happened. His best friend, Camden, had hit him on the playground that day. "He hit me hard—right in the face," he said. His mother tried to assure him, "I bet he didn't mean to hit you." But Steven protested, "No, Mom. He hit me hard—and it really hurt. Another kid had to get a teacher for me because it hurt so much." His mother was at a loss for words. All she could say was, "I'm sorry that happened to you."

The next afternoon, Steven ran to the car waving a piece of paper. "Mom, Mom," he cried breathlessly as he jumped into his booster seat. "You won't believe this! Look what Camden made for me." His mother looked at the paper. Camden, who is only five, had drawn Steven an apology. With crayons and stick figures (and probably a little help from his mother), he said he was sorry for what he had done. "This is awesome," his mother said teary-eyed. Then Steven added, "And you know what the best part was, Mom? Camden and I played together the whole time at recess—and we totally had fun today." Through Camden's apology and Steven's forgiveness, a friendship had been restored.

You restore my strength, says Psalm 23, or *You restore my soul.* How does God restore our strength, our soul? Chiefly through the forgiveness of our sins.

I said earlier that Psalm 23 is often attributed

to David the king of Israel. David knew a lot about sin. Not only did he commit adultery with Bathsheba, the wife of Uriah, but he also ordered Uriah to be killed to cover up his sin. But the prophet Nathan, learning of David's sins, marched straight into the palace and boldly confronted the king. And how did David respond? He didn't slay Nathan on the spot as he could have done. No, he hung his head in shame and said to the prophet, "I have sinned against the Lord." David humbly acknowledged his sin and repented.

David's sin was great. No doubt about it. But his trust in God was greater. So strong and so personal was that trust, he believed not even grave sin could separate him from his Shepherd. In his book *Crossing the Desert,* Father Joseph Creedon writes about sin and forgiveness. Alluding to the raising of Lazarus, he says we must, with faith and humility, identify our sins, our "personal tombs": hatred, laziness, addiction, greed, jealousy, anger, lust, self-righteousness, gossip, deceitfulness. He says, "There is no personal tomb so deep that God cannot roll back the stone and call us into the light."

God's forgiveness of us lies at the heart of Jesus' teachings. His parable of the prodigal son magnificently exemplifies God's eagerness to forgive us. While the returning son "was still a long way off," his father "caught sight of him, and was filled with compassion." The father ran to him, embraced him, put a fine robe on him, slipped a ring on his finger, welcomed him home, and threw a big party for him. All these little details demonstrate the restorative power of the father's (and God's) forgiveness.

But sometimes we are reluctant to ask God for forgiveness. We might think, "My sin is too great." Or "My sin is too small." Or "It's been so long since I went to confession I don't even know where to start." Another story might help here. A certain young man had seriously sinned against his father. He wanted to return home but he was too ashamed to make the journey. Hearing of this, the father sent his son this message: "Come as far as you can—even if it is only one step toward me. And I'll come the rest of the way to meet you." This is what God says to us too.

God restores our soul through forgiveness.

But God also asks us to do one crucial and difficult thing: We must forgive others just as God has forgiven us. This is perhaps the most challenging mandate Jesus gave us. It's so challenging we sometimes come up with all kinds of excuses for why we can't do it. We say we can't forgive because our hurt is too great. But forgiveness doesn't deny the hurt. Or we say we can't forgive because what was done against us was so wrong. Forgiveness doesn't deny the wrong either. When we forgive another, we are acknowledging that the person who offended us is more than the offense he or she has committed. As the writer Richard Foster said: "Forgiveness means that the power of love that holds us together is greater than the power of the offense that separates us."

You restore my strength. You restore my soul. It is mainly the power of God's forgiveness and our own forgiving of others that bring about this beautiful restoration.

QUESTIONS

1. Jesus' teaching on forgiveness is beautifully illustrated in the parable of the prodigal son (Luke

15:11–32). When you reflect on this parable, what words or phrases stand out for you? Why?

---

2. Recall a time when you were challenged to forgive someone for what they did. What made forgiveness so difficult? If you were able to forgive, what factors enabled you to do so? If you haven't been able to forgive, what is preventing you?

PRAYER

Watchful Shepherd,
when I am weak,
you restore my strength.
When I am weary,
you restore my soul.
When I am lost,
you find me.
When I am cast down,
you raise me up.
When I have sinned,
you extend your forgiveness.
Remind me, when I have strayed,
I need not make the whole journey
    back home to you.

I need take only one step toward you,
and you will run the rest of the way to meet me,
reclaiming me as your child.
Forgiving Shepherd,
help me in turn to forgive all
   who have wronged me.
Help me to see that the power of love
that holds us together
   is greater than the power of the offense
   that separates us.
   I ask these things through Jesus who,
   as he hung dying on the cross, prayed:
   "Father, forgive them,
   for they know not what they do." Amen.

SIX

You guide me along the right path for the sake of your name

LEADING AS JESUS LEADS

No other livestock requires more attention and careful handling than sheep. That's due mainly to two characteristics of sheep. First, sheep tend to be creatures of habit. Left to themselves they will graze in the same pasture until they have turned it into a barren wasteland. The wise shepherd knows that movement is essential for maintaining a healthy flock. And movement necessitates guidance.

The second characteristic of sheep that makes them "labor intensive" is this: they like to wander from the flock for no apparent reason. Once again it is the shepherd's responsibility to prevent them from wandering or, if they do roam, to locate them and bring them back to the flock.

This verse from Psalm 23 focuses on the shepherd's guidance and leadership: *you guide me along the right path for the sake of your name.* Other translations say you *lead* me. The words *guide* and *lead* connote the shepherd's wise and attentive direction.

The question arises, *how* does the shepherd move his sheep? When cowboys want to move a herd of cattle, they get behind the cattle and push their herd forward. But sheep are not cattle. They resist being pushed from behind. Instead, they prefer to be *led* from the front.

In John's gospel, Jesus referred to himself as the Good Shepherd. This analogy speaks volumes about how Jesus leads. Jesus isn't behind us yelling, "Go! Go!" He stands and walks ahead of us bidding, "Come! Come!" By reflecting on how

Jesus leads in the gospels, we can gain insights into how he continues to lead us today. We can also learn how we are being called to lead others.

First of all, *Jesus led gently.* He extended invitations rather than issued ultimatums. He didn't force individuals to do things. When he called his first apostles, for example, he said to them, "Come, follow me," leaving them free to come or not. When he invited the rich man to "go, sell what you have, and give to the poor," he left the man free to walk away—which the man did. Jesus was gentle with the woman with the hemorrhage, with the adulteress, with the demoniac, with Nicodemus who was too afraid to come to him during the day, with small children, and with the thief hanging on the cross beside him on Calvary.

Jesus led patiently. At times his disciples challenged his teachings. Remember Peter saying to Jesus, "Lord, if my brother sins against me, how often must I forgive him? As many as seven times?" Other times the apostles missed the point of his teachings. Despite Jesus' words on humble service (and his stellar example!), the apostles regularly vied for positions of honor.

Though Jesus expressed exasperation at times, he never gave up on his disciples. He continued to love them, instruct them, and lead them— even after their betrayal and his resurrection.

Jesus' leadership entailed self-sacrifice. His preaching and teaching must have exhausted him at times. After all, he travelled from town to town on foot. Yet he retained energy and enthusiasm for his mission. When he encountered interruptions in his schedule or his plans, he was flexible, negotiating these inconveniences with considerable grace. Some of his teachings aroused the ire of his enemies and cost him followers, yet he persevered. By eating with sinners, he sacrificed even his good reputation. And finally, his loyalty to his mission and to his Father ultimately cost him the supreme sacrifice: his very life.

Jesus led by example. He taught inclusive love and lived it, welcoming all kinds of individuals into the sweep of his love. He taught the importance of prayer, and he himself regularly sneaked off by himself to pray. Jesus taught forgiveness— even of one's enemies. As he hung on the cross, he forgave the individuals who were putting him to death. And after the resurrection, he forgave his disciples who had deserted him in his hour of greatest need.

And finally, *Jesus inspired people with his vision.* I like what the French writer Antoine de Saint-Exupery said about inspiring others: "If you want to build a ship, don't herd people together to collect wood and don't assign them tasks and work, but rather teach them to long for the endless immensity of the sea." That's what Jesus did. He tapped into people's deep longings for love, goodness, truth, beauty, peace, and, ultimately, for God.

Jesus called his vision the kingdom of God or the reign of God. It is a world where the hungry are fed, the sick are healed, the naked are clothed, and the dead are raised to new life. It is a place of peace, fellowship, nourishment, fun, and immense joy—like a wedding feast. Jesus' vision of what the world could be captivated his listeners. What's more, Jesus laid out a plan to make that vision a reality. This plan is described in his parables as well as his teachings—especially the Beatitudes.

Jesus leads us today in the same way: gently,

patiently, selflessly, by his example, and by inspiring us with his vision of the reign of God. Periodically it is good for us to appraise the way we lead others whether we are parents or grandparents, teachers or coaches, whether we are at work or at our parish, whether we serve on committees or hold some sort of office. We can ask ourselves: Are we demanding or gentle? Are we brusque or patient? Are we selfish or selfless? Do we lead by our words only or by our own example? And finally, do we inspire others with our own vision of the reign of God?

Questions

1. This chapter lists several qualities of Jesus' leadership. Which quality or qualities do you appreciate the most? Why? Which do you need to develop the most in yourself?

2. Think of someone in your life who displayed leadership qualities similar to those of Jesus—a parent, grandparent, teacher, coach, pastor, boss, coworker, friend, etc. What effect did this person's leadership style have on you? Why?

Prayer

Good Shepherd,
guide me, lead me;
go before me
and show me the way, the right path to follow.
Help me to put aside all bad habits
that lead only to barren wastelands.
Curb my wandering,
that takes me away from you
and the companionship of my fellow believers.
Be gentle with me;
be patient.
Inspire me with your teachings
and the example of your complete selflessness.
Share with me your vision of the reign of God.
Inspire me to work to make that vision a reality.
And finally, dear Shepherd,
help me to lead others as you are leading me.
Amen.

SEVEN

Even when I walk through a dark valley, I fear no harm for you are at my side.

TRUSTING GOD AMID PAIN AND DARKNESS

When summer came to ancient Palestine, a major change was in store for the sheep. The shepherd would lead his sheep on a long journey into the high country where the melting snows were beginning to expose lush expanses of green. This annual trek up into the mountains, though absolutely necessary, was filled with danger. Along the way the shepherd and sheep would encounter steep inclines, narrow trails, and deep valleys that received little sunlight. In addition, lurking behind the rocks and bushes were predators waiting to pounce. At night, without the safety of their enclosure, the sheep would be especially vulnerable. But the shepherd had traveled this path before. He knew it well. And he would be watching out for his sheep every step of the way.

Even when I walk through a dark valley. The King James translation says *the shadow of death.* Psalm 23, then, doesn't paint a utopian picture of life. This verse in particular reminds us that life can be very difficult at times, a dark valley. Phyllis Ferguson of Chardon, Ohio, knows all about the dark valleys of life.

It was February 27, 2012, an ordinary Monday in the small town of Chardon. Phyllis had just dropped off her sixteen-year-old son Demetrius at the high school. Then she drove across the street to attend the 7:30 Mass. I was there that morning too. In fact, Phyllis sat across the aisle from me. At the Sign of Peace we exchanged smiles and waves. That's when we began to hear sirens. Lots of them. They were loud and close by. After Communion, someone went up to Father at the altar and whispered something. Father looked shocked. He announced, "There's been a shooting at the high school." Later we learned the terrible details. A sixteen-year-old boy had opened fire on students in the school cafeteria. He shot six students, three of them fatally. One of the students killed was Demetrius, Phyllis's son.

I don't know how Phyllis got through this awful tragedy. Afterwards she said her faith in God and the help of family and friends sustained her. A year later, a local newspaper did a follow-up on the shooting. The article had a picture of Phyllis clutching a photo of Demetrius. She spoke about donating her son's organs when he died. She said, "Demetrius was a giving, sharing person." She added, "Even through the darkness of the situation, there was a marvelous light. Demetrius gave life to others after his death."

We may not experience dark valleys as dramatic as Phyllis's was, but we still experience them: We lose our job, or our house burns down, or we are forced to declare bankruptcy, or our son is arrested, or our spouse wants out of the marriage, or we lose our best friend to cancer, or our parent is diagnosed with Alzheimer's, or we are told the tumor is inoperable.

Not everyone passes through their personal dark valley. Some seem to get stuck in the valley. They allow the loss or catastrophe or trauma to define them as individuals. They either refuse to move on or seem powerless to do so. But one of the most important words in this verse of Psalm 23 is the word *through.* It reminds us the dark valley is a place we pass through. It is not our permanent residence. The challenge is to acknowledge our pain, hurt, and even anger when we are in a dark valley. At the same time, we are called to keep moving forward. This movement can take time—even years. It often involves the help of family, friends, professionals, and (of course) God.

The dark valleys we experience in life, as difficult as they are, can bring about good. In my book *With the Dawn Rejoicing: A Christian Perspective on Pain and Suffering,* I spoke of some of the good things that can come forth from our pain. I wrote, "None of us lives a pain-free life...Pain is universal." It is precisely because pain is universal that "it has the power to unite us as nothing else can—not even our joy." This is one reason why support groups such as Alcoholics Anonymous, Cancer Survivors, and bereavement groups are so effective. They unite people in their common pain. Individuals draw strength from others who are walking through the same dark valley.

Our pain can also be a "wise advisor." It can tell us something we may need to hear: "Slow down…let go already…spend more time with your family…listen to your body…take one day at a time…enlarge your world…reach out to her… appreciate what you have…rearrange your priorities…trust in God…forgive." Pain and adversity also have the power to bring forth qualities in us we might not otherwise develop—qualities such as patience, compassion, understanding, humility, courage, generosity, and intimacy with God.

When it comes to walking through a dark valley, Jesus has indeed been there. Like us, he experienced the ordinary trials of daily living: misunderstandings, inconveniences, hard work, disappointments, uncertainty, setbacks, worry, fatigue, loneliness. He also experienced the major adversities of life: the death of a loved one, betrayal, abandonment, terror, prolonged physical agony, and death. During our life we will not be asked to suffer what Jesus himself has not suffered in one form or another.

As the shepherd leads his sheep to higher ground, he is fully aware of what awaits his flock—those lush green expanses where they will find delight and nourishment. The sheep, on the other hand, may have no idea where they're going. But they trust the shepherd. That's all that matters. Similarly, we may not know where life is taking us. But if we know and trust the shepherd, nothing else matters.

QUESTIONS

1. Recall a time when you experienced a dark valley. Describe the circumstances. How long did it last? What helped you get through it? What effect did this experience have on you?

2. Has your pain ever been a "wise advisor" for you? If so, what wise counsel did it give you?

PRAYER

Good Shepherd,
lead me to higher ground,
where delight and nourishment await me.
Lead me up steep inclines, over narrow trails,
through dark valleys that seldom see the sun.
Though I am unsure of the destination,
I trust in you.
Though I may be afraid,
I trust in you.
Reassure me that when I am in pain,
I am never alone.
I have you.
Remind me of the goodness
that can spring forth from deep darkness:
wise counsel, union with others,
and qualities of patience, compassion, humility,
understanding, courage, and love.
Good Shepherd, I ask for these things
through Jesus, so well-acquainted
    with human pain,
and the Holy Spirit, so eager to lead me
    to higher ground.
Amen.

EIGHT

Your rod and staff give me courage

SELF-DISCIPLINE AND PERSEVERANCE: REMEMBERING WHAT WE REALLY WANT

I n ancient Israel, shepherds traveled light. But most shepherds carried two tools essential for their work: a staff and a rod. The shepherd's staff or crook, ordinarily made from wood, served as a walking stick. It was also used by the shepherd to gently pull sheep from brambles or to draw them close to check for illness or injuries. He also used the staff to guide the sheep along the right path.

The other tool was a rod. This powerful stick was a weapon the shepherd hurled at predators that threatened his flock. On occasions the shepherd would also use the rod to discipline a sheep. A few taps with the rod would let a sheep know it was getting out of line.

The psalmist says that the rod and staff *give me courage.* Another translation says they *comfort me.* Courage comes from knowing we are being protected by the shepherd. Comfort comes from experiencing God's particular care for us. We know that, even if we do stray, God will lead us back.

When we think of the rod, we ordinarily think of discipline. We recall the old adage "Spare the rod and spoil the child." But discipline is not to be equated with physical punishment. Good parents know there are other forms of discipline that are effective: giving a child a "time out" or temporarily taking away a certain privilege. But what is the goal of parental discipline? Fred Rogers, creator of the children's TV show *Mr. Rogers' Neighborhood,* said discipline is "the process of helping a child learn self-discipline."

My favorite definition of self-discipline was given by David Campbell: "Self-discipline is remembering what you want." I like to add it is remembering what you *really* want. Self-discipline is self-control *in the present* for the sake of something we really want *in the future.* It is giving up something in the short-term for the sake of a long-term goal or vision. If the vision of what we want is clear and the desire to attain it is deep, then we have a good chance of achieving our goal.

Athletes, for example, train rigorously for many years for the chance to compete in the Olympics. From time to time they actually visualize themselves standing on the podium and receiving their medal. Dieters sometimes put a photo of their younger slimmer self on their refrigerator door as a visual reminder of their goal. When they are tempted to raid the refrigerator, the photo reminds them of what they really want. Educators sponsor alumni career days where successful graduates speak to the students, thus offering them a potential vision of themselves in the future. It is a vision that can encourage the students to stay in school and do the hard work involved in pursuing a particular career.

We all have goals in life that require self-discipline. But we might want to ask ourselves: As Christians, what is our ultimate goal? The answer is simple: to become a more loving person. No more, no less. It is to persevere in loving God, self, and others. This is what Jesus taught. It is also what Jesus lived. In the end we will be judged not on how many medals we won, how many promotions we earned, or how much money we made. We will be judged on how well we loved. And loving takes perseverance.

I like the adage that says, "Persevere! Remember the great oak tree was once a little nut that held its ground." In one sense, every oak tree is simply an acorn that persevered. But it didn't persevere in remaining an acorn. Over time the little nut was radically transformed into a majestic tree. Using this metaphor, we can say that God calls us not to remain the same through sheer stubbornness. Rather, God calls us to radical transformation into the person of Jesus through persevering love.

On many occasions Jesus encouraged his disciples to persevere. In explaining the parable of the sower, for example, Jesus said that the seed that fell on rich soil represented those who, upon hearing the word of God, "hold it fast in an honest and good heart, and bear fruit with patient enduring." Jesus encouraged self-discipline too. "Take up your cross and follow me," he said. It is interesting to note that the etymology of the words *discipline* and *disciple* is the same: the Latin *discipulus*, meaning student or instruction.

Jesus possessed great self-discipline. He persevered in his public ministry despite personal fatigue, the lack of understanding of some of his closest followers, and the growing antagonism of certain religious leaders. What was the source of such strength? To answer this, we must go back to his baptism in the Jordan River. Something happened there that gave direction to Jesus' entire life. As he came up out of the water that day, Jesus had a profound religious experience. The heavens opened up and he saw a dove descending upon him. Then he heard a voice from the heavens saying, "This is my beloved Son, with whom I am well pleased." Jesus experienced divine affirmation. He knew he was loved by God. Personally. Uniquely. Unconditionally. It was precisely this conviction that enabled him to persevere in his mission all the way to Calvary. We might ask ourselves: Do we really believe we are God's beloved son or daughter?

Max Lucado has written a little book for children entitled *God Thinks You're Wonderful*. I often use it for talks and retreats, because I know adults need to hear its message too. The book says things like this: "God is fond of you...If God had a wallet, your picture would be in it...If God had a refrigerator, your picture would be on it... Whenever you want to talk, God will listen... Face it, friend, God is crazy about you."

QUESTIONS

1. Recall a time when you had to practice self-discipline. What made your self-discipline hard? Did "remembering what you really want" help you to persevere in achieving your goal?

2. Do you really believe you are loved personally, uniquely, and unconditionally by God? If so, what leads you to believe this? If not, what prevents you from believing this?

PRAYER

Caring Shepherd,
your staff and rod give me courage.
With them you protect me,
you lift me up,
you guide me on the right path.
Your rod and staff give me comfort.
I know if I get stuck in brambles,
you will set me free.
If I lose my way,
you will find me and bring me home again.
Persevering Shepherd,
help me always to remember what I *really* want:
to become a more loving person.
Let me hear those same words
you spoke to Jesus:
"You are my beloved son (daughter)
in whom I am well pleased."
Convince me: You are crazy about me.
Amen.

NINE

You set a table before me as my enemies watch

BIBLICAL HOSPITALITY: WELCOMING THE MYSTERY OF LIFE

One of the traditional images of God in Scripture is God as gracious host. This verse from Psalm 23 is rooted in that tradition, for it depicts God setting before us a nourishing meal. Notice that God serves that meal as our "enemies watch." This could mean that God nourishes us not merely when our "enemies" (that is, our adversities, temptations, or crises) are far away from us. Rather, God nourishes us even in the midst of threatening circumstances. Our lives don't have to be problem-free for God to show up.

This image of God as a hospitable host is certainly a comforting one. But it is also a demanding one. For God's gracious hospitality toward us calls us to show gracious hospitality toward others.

In fact, the practice of hospitality was so important for the ancient Israelites, it was inscribed in their law. In Deuteronomy, for example, Moses (speaking for God) commands the people to show hospitality to everyone, but especially to strangers (or aliens), widows, and orphans. Why are these three types of individuals singled out? Because they all share a common plight: they are disadvantaged. Aliens, widows, and orphans had few if any legal rights in Israel. Often they had no source of income. They were essentially dependent on the generosity of others for their survival—just as the Israelites were dependent on God's generosity for their survival.

There's more. Over time the Israelites came to believe that in showing hospitality to others, they were somehow welcoming the mystery of God into their lives. This conviction is beautifully illustrated in the story of Abraham and his three mysterious visitors (Gen 18:1–15). The story is a simple one. While resting at the entrance to his tent one hot afternoon, Abraham spots three strangers off in the distance. Now he could have said, "It's too hot!" or "I'm too tired" to welcome company. But no, he runs out to them and begs them to be his guests. Extending hospitality isn't always convenient.

The strangers accept his invitation. Abraham provides water for their weary feet—a real extravagance in the middle of a desert! He then prepares a lavish meal for them—with Sarah's help, of course. Their hospitality is rewarded. For before the strangers depart, they impart a promise from God: Within a year Abraham and Sarah will have a son. Now Abraham and Sarah are "advanced in years." In fact, Sarah initially laughs at the prospect of having a baby. But the strangers remind them that nothing is "too marvelous for the Lord to do." By showing hospitality to three strangers, Abraham and Sarah had welcomed the mystery of

God into their life—and eventually, a new baby.

This theme of hospitality saturates the New Testament as well. At the Annunciation, Mary consents to bear "the Son of the Most High." Talk about hospitality! She welcomes God into her very womb! Joseph, after considerable inner turmoil, welcomes Mary and her unborn child into his life, choosing to raise the boy as his own. Mary and Joseph must have passed down this welcoming attitude to Jesus. For during his public ministry, Jesus welcomed all kinds of people into his life: Jew and Gentile, men, women, children, rich and poor, saints and sinners, the sick, outcasts, a Roman centurion, and (after the resurrection) even the friends who had betrayed him.

Jesus' parables also center on this theme of hospitality. The father welcomes back his wayward son with a magnificent party, while the Samaritan reaches out in tenderness to the mangled stranger (his enemy, no less!) on the side of the road. Later, when Jesus gives the criterion for admission into the heavenly kingdom, it is essentially the practice of hospitality: "For I was hungry and you gave me food, I was thirsty and you gave me drink, naked and you clothed me, ill and you cared for me, in prison and you visited me." Jesus adds, "Whatever you did to one of these least brothers or sisters of mine, you did for me." The "least" are essentially the disadvantaged, the marginalized of society.

At the Last Supper, Jesus once again demonstrates hospitality in a stunning way. Toward the end of the meal he dons a makeshift apron and washes the feet of his disciples, performing the ritual of hospitality usually done by a servant. Then, at this final meal of his life, Jesus sets before his disciples (and us!) a gracious feast: the Eucharist. In doing so he invites us to receive his own body and blood as sustenance for our earthly journey. And finally, in the Garden of Gethsemane, Jesus shows again his openness to all of life by embracing his crucifixion, trusting that God, Abba, would somehow extract goodness from even this horrific event. After all, "nothing is too marvelous for the Lord to do."

You set a table before me. We imitate God's gracious hospitality every time we show a welcoming attitude toward life—all of life. We begin by welcoming our particular life as a precious gift from God. We welcome the "givens" of our personal history and family. We embrace ourselves too with our talents and limitations. Hospitality means we are open even to those things over which we have little or no control: interruptions, chance happenings, accidents, historic events. For we believe that the mystery of God can be found everywhere—even in ambiguity or apparent misfortune.

Hospitality means we also "set a table" before others—especially the disadvantaged, the defenseless, and the voiceless. We welcome strangers—that is, individuals whom we do not know or who are different from ourselves. I always say that becoming a parent is one of the greatest acts of hospitality there is, because parents welcome this "little stranger" into their homes and hearts! We can dare to extend hospitality toward life because we know and trust the Author of Life. As Christians we believe that God's grace moves beneath the surface of ordinary life.

QUESTIONS

1. List some of the "givens" you have had to accept or even welcome in your life. Have any of these "givens" turned out to be obvious blessings for you? How?

---

2. Who are the aliens, the disadvantaged, and the defenseless in our world today? How can you show them hospitality?

PRAYER

Almighty God, you serve me?
Shouldn't it be the other way around?
Shouldn't I be serving you?
And yet, that is what your sacred word says:
you set a table before me.
You bid me welcome. *You* serve *me.*
Divine Host, you welcomed me into being
and continue to welcome me every day
    of my life.
You nourish me in ways too numerous to count,
too wondrous to name, too deep to fathom.
You nourish me "in the sight of my enemies":
my adversities, temptations, crises.

My life need not be problem-free
for you to be at the heart of it.
Hospitable One,
you bid me to welcome life—all of life,
especially my own particular life.
You bid me to welcome others
    just as you welcome me—
especially those who are disadvantaged
    in any way.
Give me insight to see that in welcoming life
    and others
I am welcoming the mystery of who you are.
I ask for these things through Jesus,
the Welcoming One. Amen.

TEN

You anoint my head with oil

TENDING THE WOUNDS OF ONE ANOTHER

My brother John was very ill. The cancer was now in his brain. On Sunday, while I was visiting him in his home, he said he would like to be anointed. I told him I would get a priest from our parish to come and anoint him the next day. But I had forgotten that all the priests in the diocese were out of town for a three-day meeting with the bishop. There were no priests around. Monday, after a communion service at our church, I described my predicament to our deacon, who knew John well. He led me into the sacristy, handed me the sacred oil and the book of prayers, and said, "Melannie, you anoint your brother." And so I did. Early the next morning, I drove to John's again. He was clearly dying now, but still conscious. I prayed a few of the prayers from the book, prayed a few words of my own, and then anointed John by tracing a cross on his forehead with the oils. Then I passed the oils to his wife, Mary, and to his son, John. And they both anointed him too. About ten minutes later John took his final breath.

You anoint my head with oil. These words have special meaning for me now—ever since, due to circumstances, I was privileged to anoint my brother with the sacred oil just minutes before he slipped into eternity.

From ancient times, people have used oil for healing. They massaged oil into aching muscles. They rubbed oil onto chapped skin. And they poured oil over cuts and bruises to soothe their pain. Yes, even shepherds carried a flask of oil to facilitate the healing of wounds on their sheep.

In Scripture, we find many examples of people being anointed with oil—but not merely for healing purposes. The prophet Samuel, for example, anoints Saul as the first king of Israel. In this case the oil signifies that the anointed one has been consecrated for a particular task.

Some of the sacraments employ oil (sacred chrism) as part of their ritual. At baptism, we are anointed with oil as a sign of our initiation into Christian discipleship. In fact, the word *Christian* means *anointed.* At confirmation, we are once again anointed with oil to signify our sharing more completely in the mission of Jesus. And when we receive the sacrament of the anointing of the sick, our hands and forehead are anointed with blessed oil as the priest prays, "Through this holy anointing may the Lord in his love and mercy help you with the grace of the Holy Spirit."

During his earthly life, Jesus was widely proclaimed as a healer. The four gospels are filled with stories of his many cures. He cures Peter's mother-in-law, a man with a withered hand, a woman bent over for eighteen years, a man born blind, ten lepers, a woman suffering from a hemorrhage, a paralytic, a man possessed by demons—and the list goes on. He even raises three individuals from death: the daughter of Jairus, the son of the widow of Nain, and his good friend Lazarus. Sickness and death moved Jesus to compassion. But as we follow his public life, we notice something. The closer Jesus gets to Calvary, the more infrequent the healings become. What's going on here?

Some theologians say that as Jesus grew in his understanding of his mission, he realized he was sent not to take away people's physical pain and suffering—though he could. Rather, he was sent to *embrace* human pain and suffering himself and thus teach us that they can be redemptive. As Paul Claudel wrote, "Jesus came not to eradicate our pain, but to fill it with his presence."

This doesn't mean that we shouldn't pray for physical healing. After all, our faith encourages us to pray for what we believe we need. And amazingly, healing miracles still occur. But we must always bear in mind that spiritual health is more important than physical health. And eternal life far outweighs this earthly existence.

Sometimes our wounds are not physical, but psychological or spiritual. Perhaps we have been mistreated or even abused. Like physical wounds, these interior wounds must be tended to before they fester into resentment and bitterness. Do we take our wounds to God in our prayer? If necessary, do we seek help—a counselor, spiritual director, or friend?

Our own need for healing can make us more sensitive to others who struggle with health issues and psychological wounds. We can reach out to them in small but meaningful ways. Jesus told a magnificent parable about reaching out to those in pain, the parable of the good Samaritan (Luke 10:29–37). The victim in the parable was lying on the side of the road after being robbed and beaten by thugs. Both the priest and Levite notice the man but pass him by—perhaps because of fear. But the Samaritan, the victim's enemy, is moved with compassion at the sight of the stranger. Putting aside his own agenda, fears, and prejudices, he reaches out to the man with extraordinary tenderness, even pouring oil over his wounds. The parable highlights the supreme importance of compassion—that is, the capacity to live inside another's skin.

You anoint my head with oil. God comforts us. God heals us. But as the Protestant preacher J. H. Jowett wrote: "God does not comfort us to make us comfortable, but to make us comforters." This brief story illustrates this point. A little girl came home late from school. "Why are you late?" her mother asked her angrily. She said, "I had to help a girl who was in trouble." Her mother asked, "What did you do to help her?" She replied, "I sat down next to her and helped her cry."

QUESTIONS

1. Think of a time when you were moved with compassion toward another. What aroused your compassion? What did your compassion move you to do?

2. How do you tend your own wounds? Do you take them to God in prayer? Do you seek help from others?

PRAYER

Loving Shepherd,
you anoint my head with oil.
You ease my irritations;
you calm my spirit;
you heal my wounds.
By your tender care
you remind me: I belong to you.
You consecrate me for my life's special mission:
witnessing to your love, truth, and beauty
wherever I may be.
I thank you for the daily anointing
    of your healing grace.
May I in turn reach out to others
who struggle with ill health,
    psychological bruises,
and wounds of all kinds.
I ask for these things through Jesus
and the power of his healing Spirit.
Amen.

ELEVEN

My cup overflows

CULTIVATING THE ATTITUDE
OF GRATITUDE

I n ancient Israel, where hospitality was valued so highly, a gracious host always filled the guest's cup of wine to the brim—almost to overflowing. The host would keep filling the cup to the brim as a sign that the host didn't want his guest to leave.

My cup overflows. Three little words. Yet they are an expression of immense gratitude, uttered by someone in touch with the giftedness of life. Rabbi Harold Kushner calls gratitude "the funda-

77

mental religious emotion. It is where religion begins in the human heart." G. K. Chesterton, the great British writer, would agree. Raised without religion, he claimed he found his way to God because he needed someone to thank.

Many Christians pray grace before meals as a way of thanking God for the gift of food. One traditional form of grace is this: "Bless us, O Lord, and these thy gifts which we are about to receive from thy bounty, through Christ our Lord. Amen." It's the phrase *from thy bounty* that gives me pause here. Theologians tell us we can learn things about God by studying the natural world. Creation, in other words, reflects the Creator. One thing we learn from gazing at creation is this: Our God is a God of bounty. Take the stars, for example. God didn't create just a few stars or even a few million stars. Our Milky Way galaxy contains over one hundred million stars! And there are at least one hundred billion other galaxies! And each one of these galaxies contains between ten million and one trillion stars! Talk about bounty!

And God got carried away with color too. The

human eye can distinguish a few million different colors, hues, shades, and tints. And what about different tastes? Pronounce the following words slowly. As you say each one, imagine the particular taste indicated by each word: apple, orange, celery, tomato, strawberry, blueberry, sweetcorn, peanuts, vanilla, chocolate. Have you thanked God for the gifts of color and taste lately?

Some Christians don't restrict saying grace to meal time. I know people who say a brief prayer of thanksgiving before other activities in their day: before getting out of bed in the morning, before taking a shower or bath, before driving their car, before starting a meeting, before reading a book, before beginning a project, before watching a movie, before going for a walk, and before going to bed. This practice reminds us that everything is gift. And it challenges us to look for blessings in everything we do—even the mundane or difficult.

Gratitude is an attitude. It's a way of looking at the world. Studies show that a grateful person tends to be a happy person. We are not born grateful though. How many times do parents have to coax their small children to say "thank you" after receiving a cookie or other treat? Thankfully, gratitude can be learned and cultivated. What's more, gratitude seems to beget gratitude. The very act of saying "thank you" makes us more aware of other gifts we have received.

Gratitude is an attitude that must be deliberately chosen despite the evidence that threatens to pull us toward bitterness, despair, and cynicism. Many countries have set aside a specific day of the year for giving thanks—often at harvest time. In the United States, Thanksgiving Day was declared a holiday by President Abraham Lincoln on October 3, 1863. That was in the middle of the devastating Civil War! There's a lesson for us even here: We don't have to wait for ideal circumstances to give thanks. The challenge is to give thanks even during difficult and painful times.

We believe that God is present in our lives all the time, not merely in the so-called "good times." Our faith tells us God is at work in sun and darkness, pleasure and pain, harmony and dissonance. We thank God, then, not just because things work out the way we want them to work out. No, we thank God for being a God who, from messiness, brings forth beauty; from absurdity, new meaning; and from death, everlasting life. Venerable Solanus Casey, a simple Capuchin friar, used to say, "Thank God ahead of time." Now that takes great faith!

Brother David Steindl-Rast, a Benedictine monk from Elmira, NY, has written and lectured extensively on gratitude. According to him, thanks-*giving* must include thanks-*living*. He maintains it is not enough to thank God for the gifts we have received. We must *do something* with these gifts. If we have good health, for example, we can use that health to help someone with failing health. If we are good with children, we can offer to babysit for a frazzled parent. If we are blessed with a little extra time, we can visit someone who is homebound or in prison. If we have an abundance of food, we can donate items to a local food pantry. If we have been blessed with an education, we can help educate someone else—by listening to a child read, by helping a student with homework, or by contributing to our high school or college scholarship fund.

In short, *doing* thanks is the best way of *giving* thanks.

Recently I saw a bumper sticker that said: IM BLSST. I think that's just another way of saying, "My cup overflows."

Questions

1. *Appraise your "gratitude attitude" for one day. How often you say "thank you" to someone—including God? How often does someone say "thank you" to you?*

2. *What are some of your gifts that you are thankful for? How do you use these gifts to help others?*

Prayer

Bountiful God,
my cup overflows.
My cup overflows with the abundance
  of your creation:
stars, oceans, mountains, forests,
flowers, insects, birds, and animals of all kinds,
colors, tastes, aromas, sounds, and feelings.

Thank you. Thank you.
My cup overflows with the goodness of people:
family and friends, colleagues
    and acquaintances;
teachers, health care personnel, caregivers,
    safety providers,
religious leaders, and all who serve
    the needs of others.
Thank you. Thank you.
My cup overflows with signs of your love
    for me, for us:
your holy word, Jesus your Son, the Holy Spirit,
prayer, Eucharist, forgiveness, song,
insights, consolations, challenges,
    and graces of all kinds.
Thank you. Thank you.
Bountiful God,
my cup overflows.
Help me to share the abundance
    of my gifts with others,
transforming my thanks-*giving*
    into thanks-*living.*
Amen.

Only goodness and love will pursue me all the days of my life

BEING PURSUED BY GOD

O nly goodness and love will pursue me all the days of my life. This verse from Psalm 23 restates the conviction we heard earlier in the psalm: No matter what happens in our life, God is somehow in the mix. But this line adds something more to that conviction. The King James translation says: *Surely goodness*

and mercy shall follow me all the days of my life.
Notice that word *surely.* The psalmist doesn't say
maybe or *possibly* or even *I hope.* No, he says
surely. He is absolutely certain.

What I also like about this verse is the verb
will pursue me. It is much stronger than *shall
follow me.* Eugene Peterson, in *The Message,*
translates this line: *Your beauty and love chase
after me every day of my life.* Earlier in this psalm
we saw that God leads us. But this line says God
pursues or even chases us too.

We sometimes think of the spiritual life as
our pursuit of God—as if God is hiding from us
and it is our job to seek and find God. Though
there's an element of truth in that image, it is far
more accurate to describe our relationship with
God in this way: God seeks us first! As St. John
wrote: "We love [God] because [God] loved us
first." A striking poetic description of God as
pursuer is found in Francis Thompson's poem
"The Hound of Heaven." In this poem the nar-
rator is running away from God. He says, "I fled
him down the nights and down the days." But
God, like a good hunting hound, pursues him

"with unhurried chase/And unperturbed pace."

I find great consolation in knowing that God is pursuing me, that God is pursuing all of us. In my travels, I often meet parents who are worried about their adult children who no longer go to church or practice their faith. I remind these parents, "God deeply desires a relationship with your son or daughter. God is pursuing them. God is relentless in loving them. Trust in God's relentless pursuing." I also remind them that God comes to us in a wide variety of ways: "The way God comes to you may not be the same way God comes to your children." I conclude by telling the parents there are only three things they can do in this regard: 1) continue to love their children, 2) pray for them, and 3) live their own life of faith with love, devotion, and joy.

Only goodness and love will pursue me all the days of my life. How consoling these words are! At the same time, they are challenging. (It seems God's consolations always include a challenge!) If God's goodness and love pursue me, then do I in turn extend my goodness and love to others? And who are these others? The old proverb says,

"Charity begins at home." Our love and goodness must first be extended to those closest to us: our spouse, our family, our fellow community members, our friends, our coworkers. Loving these individuals can be challenging because we know them so well—which means we know their faults, failings, and irritating idiosyncrasies. In addition, these individuals are such a part of our daily life that we can easily take them for granted.

In her book *Jesus, CEO,* Laurie Beth Jones describes what she calls "The Sprinkler Phenomenon of Management." She says if you look at a sprinkler head in a lawn, you sometimes see that the grass immediately around the head is brown. Ironically, the grass closest to the source of the water often gets no water, whereas the grass farther away gets plenty of water and flourishes. Jones maintains that some managers overlook or ignore the people closest to them. I think this phenomenon also applies to those of us trying to live the Christian mandate to love. In our loving, we too sometimes overlook the people closest to us. We pour out our love on others—the people we serve through our work or ministry, for example, or the neighbors down the street—while overlooking the very individuals we live with or work beside every day.

The people we are challenged to love also include those individuals we find difficult to love. Dorothy Day, co-founder of *The Catholic Worker*, lived and worked at a soup kitchen and homeless shelter in one of the poorest sections of New York City. In her journals she describes how hard it was for her at times to love the men and women who came for help. In order to love those individuals she found unpleasant or even malevolent, she begged for God's help. Her example reminds us to be patient with our efforts to love more inclusively and to ask God for help.

The last part of this line says *all the days of my life.* There is goodness and love (and beauty and mercy) in every day—in the here and now, in this situation, with these individuals—no matter how unpromising or tough the circumstances may seem. This doesn't mean we always immediately *see* that goodness and love. But sometimes, when we look back upon the difficult times, we see how God was indeed there bringing about goodness. As St. Paul wrote, "We know that all things work for good for those who love God." This is the conviction of the author of Psalm 23. Is it our conviction too?

QUESTIONS

1. Have you ever experienced difficulty living the words "Charity begins at home"? What helps you to be loving and patient with the people you live or work with?

2. Does the image of a pursuing God frighten you or comfort you? Why?

PRAYER

Loving God, you pursue me.
You pursue all of us.
And in your pursuing you carry within yourself
goodness and love, beauty and mercy.
Surely this is true.
Your goodness and love
pursue me all the days of my life.
Not merely the "good days"
    but the "bad ones" too,

not merely the easy days but the tough ones
  as well.
No matter what my circumstances,
you are in the mix.
"Reality is your home address."
Help me to extend my own goodness and love,
beauty and mercy, to everyone I meet every day:
family, friends, coworkers, strangers.
Help me to love those individuals
I find difficult to love. (You know who they are.)
Give me patience and strength
to do the hard work of loving unconditionally,
as you love me, as you love us.
I ask for these things through Jesus
and the power of his pursuing Spirit. Amen.

THIRTEEN

And I will dwell in the house of the Lord for years to come

GLIMPSING HEAVEN ON EARTH

Psalm 23 began with a confident declaration: *The Lord is my shepherd.* That little word *my* implies an intimate relationship: I belong to the shepherd and the shepherd belongs to me. Psalm 23 ends with another bold statement: *I will dwell in the house of the Lord for years to come.* These words also suggest intimacy with God. After all, we don't enter just anybody's house. But we gladly enter the house of our friends. Notice too that the verse doesn't say I will *visit* the house of the Lord. It says I will *dwell* there. There's a permanency in this living arrangement that is reinforced by the phrase *for years to come*—or, as another translation says, *forever*.

We might ask: What is meant by *the house of the Lord*? We could equate God's house with a church, temple, mosque, or shrine. But that's probably not what is intended here. Rather, God's house more likely means God's *household*. Or better yet, God's *family*. Dwelling in God's household or family makes us beneficiaries of God's protection and good company.

Another way of looking at this word *house* is to see it as *God's presence*. The thought of dwelling in God's presence 24/7 can be either unnerving or comforting. It all depends on who God is for us. A little story illustrates this point.

A mother was watching TV in the living room. Her little four-year-old son had gone into the kitchen. All of a sudden the woman heard the lid on the cookie jar being tampered with. She called out, "Nicky, what are you doing in there?"

Silence. She heard more noise from the cookie jar. "Nicky," she called again. "Are you stealing a cookie?" Silence. Finally she said, "Remember, God is watching you!" A few moments later the little boy appeared in the living room smiling and carrying a big chocolate chip cookie in each hand. Surprised, his mother said, "Didn't I tell you God was watching you?" The boy replied, "Yes—and he told me to take two!" The mother had tried to use the presence of God to frighten the boy into NOT taking a cookie. But instead, her words made the boy take TWO cookies—because that's the God he knew!

For some people, this final verse conjures up the idea of heaven, our final home. It is good to remind ourselves on a regular basis that this earthly life—whether things are going very well or very badly—is not our final destination. The Dominican priest Timothy Radcliffe travels all over the world. When he checks in at the airport for a flight home, he is often asked, "Is London your final destination?" He says he's always tempted to reply, "No. I hope Paradise is."

A good question to ask ourselves from time to

time is this: What is our idea of heaven? (I smile when I recall St. Brigid of Ireland, a sixth-century abbess. She envisioned heaven as a large family gathered around a lake of beer!) We know what St. Paul said about heaven: "Eye has not seen, and ear has not heard, nor has it entered the human heart, what God has prepared for those who love him." In one way, then, we have no idea what heaven is like, it is so far beyond our experience. Yet I believe we are given little glimpses of heaven in our everyday experiences. Here's one such glimpse from my book *Everyday Epiphanies*. I call it "Heaven is coming home":

On my way home from the meeting I decide to stop in and see Mom and Dad. It's a cold, dark November evening. Suppertime. As I pull into the driveway I see lights on in the kitchen. Through the window I spot Dad in his red plaid flannel shirt, sitting at the table reading the newspaper. Mom, aproned, is standing by the stove stirring something— homemade leek soup, perhaps. Dad, catching sight of me through the window, smiles and stands up stiffly and slightly stooped. As I step onto the back porch, Dad opens the door wide and announces cheerfully, "Well, look who's here!" And I step into the warmth of that kitchen and into the warmth of their embraces. That's what it's going to be like when I die and enter heaven. It will be like stepping out of the cold and darkness, into the warmth and brightness of a homey kitchen, with Mom and Dad there waiting for me. And they will both smile when they see me and open wide their arms. And Dad will announce cheerfully, "Well, look who's here!"

Here are some other ordinary experiences that can be glimpses of heaven:

- celebrating a happy occasion such as a birthday, wedding, or anniversary
- standing at night beneath a canopy of stars
- being held by someone you love and who loves you
- being reunited with a long-lost friend
- strolling along the shore and being mesmerized by the crashing waves

- singing along to a favorite song
- regaining your health after a long illness
- sitting in a crowd at a sporting event and cheering madly for your team
- gazing in wonder at a newborn baby
- laughing hysterically with friends over a funny story

We sometimes describe heaven as a place of eternal happiness. But we don't have to wait until heaven to be happy—as the examples above show. The fact that we have a Shepherd who knows us, loves us, cares for us, and walks with us should put a lilt in our step and a smile on our face throughout our earthly pilgrimage. As the British writer William Barclay wrote, "A gloomy Christian is a contradiction in terms."

QUESTIONS

1. Recall an experience that was for you a glimpse of heaven. How did this experience make you feel? What effect does it still have on you?

2. Do you ever think about heaven, talk about heaven, or long for heaven? Why or why not?

Prayer

Loving God,
I belong to you and you belong to me.
I will dwell in your house for years to come.
I am a member of your household, your family.
Thus I enjoy your protection
    and your good company.
I also enjoy the good company
of all my brothers and sisters.
Thank you for all the happiness
    I have experienced
so far on my earthly journey.
And thank you for the glimpses of heaven
you have given me.
I dwell in your presence every day of my life.
May my sense of your presence
put a lilt in my step and a smile on my face.
I ask for these things through Jesus
and the power of his joyful Spirit.
Amen.

CONCLUSION

We have finished our walk through Psalm 23. What have we learned by pondering the words of this beautiful prayer? Here is a brief summary of the psalm's major themes:

The Lord is *my* Shepherd. I belong to God and God belongs to me. Nothing I do and nothing that happens to me can separate me from God.

God knows me through and through—and still loves me!

My daily conversation with God in prayer is essential for my life.

I lack nothing because I have God.

I fear nothing, for God is with me always and with those I love.

When I experience restlessness or loneliness, I know these are signs that I am made for God.

No one or nothing else can fully satisfy the deepest longings of my heart.

God calls me regularly to "Come aside and rest a while."

Celebrating the Sabbath helps forge my bonds with God and with family and community.

God provides natural and spiritual waters to sustain and refresh me.

I am called to reverence water, realizing it is a basic right for all people.

God is the great restorer of my strength and my soul—chiefly through the forgiveness of my sins.

At the heart of Jesus' life and teachings is the mandate to forgive others—even our enemies.

God guides and leads me throughout my life.

I can learn a lot about leadership by reflecting on how Jesus leads others in the gospels.

I am called to lead others with gentleness, patience, self-sacrifice, and by my own example.

When I encounter dark valleys in my life (and I will!), I know God will lead me through them.

Pain can be a wise advisor.

God can bring goodness from pain, sorrow, and even evil.

Self-discipline is remembering what I really want. Ultimately, what I really want is to become a more loving person.

By the way I live my life, by the decisions and choices I make, I can partner with God to bring about the reign of God.

God is a host who welcomes me warmly and serves me graciously.

God calls me to welcome and serve others, especially those who are disadvantaged in any way.

God anoints me with healing oil and calls me to be a healing presence for others.

God consecrates me for my special mission in life.

Gratitude is an attitude that can be cultivated.

Thanks-*giving* must include thanks-*living*.

God's goodness, love, and mercy are pursuing me every day.

I dwell in God's presence here and now and in eternity.

My spiritual bumper sticker reads: IM BLSST!